First Grade Math Workbook
Basic Addition, Subtraction, Division and Multiplication

BABY PROFESSOR
EDUCATION KIDS

Speedy Publishing LLC
40 E. Main St. #1156
Newark, DE 19711
www.speedypublishing.com

Name: _______________________________ Score: _____

1. $3 + 6 + 2 = $ _____

2. $5 + 2 + 1 = $ _____

3. $3 + 3 + 6 = $ _____

4. $2 + 3 + 5 = $ _____

5. $3 + 2 + 3 = $ _____

6. $1 + 2 + 9 = $ _____

7. $6 + 0 + 2 = $ _____

8. $1 + 9 + 4 = $ _____

Name: ________________________________ Score: ______

1. $2 + 6 + 1 = $ _____

2. $1 + 8 + 1 = $ _____

3. $2 + 0 + 9 = $ _____

4. $5 + 4 + 8 = $ _____

5. $0 + 3 + 1 = $ _____

6. $3 + 0 + 8 = $ _____

7. $3 + 4 + 2 = $ _____

8. $0 + 3 + 6 = $ _____

Name: _________________________________ Score: _______

1. 5 + 6 + 8 = _____

5. 6 + 1 + 1 = _____

2. 2 + 3 + 4 = _____

6. 0 + 3 + 2 = _____

3. 8 + 4 + 4 = _____

7. 5 + 4 + 8 = _____

4. 3 + 3 + 5 = _____

8. 5 + 5 + 3 = _____

Name: _______________________________ Score: _______

1. 9 + 5 + 1 = _____

2. 5 + 2 + 5 = _____

3. 3 + 7 + 5 = _____

4. 5 + 4 + 3 = _____

5. 5 + 3 + 7 = _____

6. 4 + 1 + 6 = _____

7. 6 + 4 + 2 = _____

8. 1 + 3 + 5 = _____

Name: ___________________________________ Score: _____

1. $1 + 2 + 7 =$ _____

2. $2 + 3 + 4 =$ _____

3. $6 + 3 + 9 =$ _____

4. $1 + 6 + 1 =$ _____

5. $0 + 4 + 9 =$ _____

6. $4 + 5 + 3 =$ _____

7. $2 + 2 + 3 =$ _____

8. $6 + 4 + 6 =$ _____

Name: _________________________________ Score: ______

1. $4 + 2 + 7 =$ _____

2. $4 + 6 + 6 =$ _____

3. $6 + 1 + 4 =$ _____

4. $4 + 1 + 6 =$ _____

5. $5 + 1 + 9 =$ _____

6. $1 + 5 + 7 =$ _____

7. $1 + 3 + 5 =$ _____

8. $2 + 6 + 2 =$ _____

ADDITION

Name: _________________________________ Score: _______

1. $3 + 3 + 6 =$ _____

2. $5 + 5 + 4 =$ _____

3. $7 + 2 + 4 =$ _____

4. $2 + 5 + 2 =$ _____

5. $6 + 9 + 5 =$ _____

6. $6 + 5 + 1 =$ _____

7. $5 + 5 + 5 =$ _____

8. $2 + 4 + 2 =$ _____

Name: _______________________________ Score: _______

1. $5 + 7 + 3 =$ _____

5. $3 + 9 + 5 =$ _____

2. $1 + 1 + 1 =$ _____

6. $5 + 4 + 3 =$ _____

3. $4 + 7 + 3 =$ _____

7. $1 + 2 + 3 =$ _____

4. $2 + 0 + 8 =$ _____

8. $6 + 5 + 9 =$ _____

Name: ______________________________ Score: _______

1. 72 – 10 = ______

2. 26 – 2 = ______

3. 86 – 4 = ______

4. 96 – 0 = ______

5. 17 – 2 = ______

6. 54 – 4 = ______

7. 18 – 8 = ______

8. 47 – 7 = ______

Name: _________________________________ Score: ______

1. 87 − 16 = ______

2. 65 − 4 = ______

3. 79 − 7 = ______

4. 86 − 13 = ______

5. 97 − 3 = ______

6. 25 − 0 = ______

7. 32 − 11 = ______

8. 47 − 3 = ______

Name: _______________________________ Score: _______

1. 35 – 0 = _______

2. 67 – 7 = _______

3. 43 – 0 = _______

4. 18 – 2 = _______

5. 39 – 2 = _______

6. 45 – 5 = _______

7. 73 – 2 = _______

8. 66 – 14 = _______

Name: _______________________________ Score: ______

1. 47 − 2 = ______

2. 48 − 7 = ______

3. 39 − 7 = ______

4. 17 − 5 = ______

5. 99 − 4 = ______

6. 17 − 15 = ______

7. 17 − 4 = ______

8. 25 − 4 = ______

Name: __________________________________ Score: ______

1. 36 – 3 = ______

2. 15 – 0 = ______

3. 88 – 1 = ______

4. 99 – 0 = ______

5. 53 – 2 = ______

6. 89 – 3 = ______

7. 59 – 0 = ______

8. 58 – 0 = ______

Name: _______________________________ Score: _______

1. 99 – 5 = _______

2. 85 – 13 = _______

3. 97 – 15 = _______

4. 26 – 6 = _______

5. 68 – 8 = _______

6. 36 – 1 = _______

7. 54 – 13 = _______

8. 27 – 5 = _______

SUBTRACTION

Name: _________________________________ Score: ______

1. 77 – 7 = ______

2. 39 – 6 = ______

3. 39 – 9 = ______

4. 76 – 5 = ______

5. 67 – 7 = ______

6. 73 – 10 = ______

7. 57 – 15 = ______

8. 22 – 1 = ______

Name: _________________________________ Score: ______

1. 69 – 8 = ______

2. 69 – 1 = ______

3. 34 – 0 = ______

4. 28 – 1 = ______

5. 53 – 3 = ______

6. 49 – 6 = ______

7. 51 – 10 = ______

8. 82 – 0 = ______

Name: _________________________________ Score: _______

1. $5 \times 9 =$ _______

2. $10 \times 5 =$ _______

3. $5 \times 4 =$ _______

4. $5 \times 6 =$ _______

5. $10 \times 10 =$ _______

6. $5 \times 5 =$ _______

7. $5 \times 2 =$ _______

8. $10 \times 4 =$ _______

Name: _________________________________ Score: _______

1. $5 \times 10 =$ _______

2. $10 \times 11 =$ _______

3. $5 \times 11 =$ _______

4. $10 \times 7 =$ _______

5. $5 \times 7 =$ _______

6. $10 \times 1 =$ _______

7. $10 \times 6 =$ _______

8. $10 \times 3 =$ _______

MULTIPLICATION

Name: _________________________________ Score: ______

1. $10 \times 9 =$ ______

2. $5 \times 8 =$ ______

3. $10 \times 2 =$ ______

4. $5 \times 12 =$ ______

5. $10 \times 10 =$ ______

6. $10 \times 2 =$ ______

7. $10 \times 7 =$ ______

8. $10 \times 6 =$ ______

Name: _________________________________ Score: _______

1. $5 \times 1 =$ _______

2. $5 \times 6 =$ _______

3. $5 \times 11 =$ _______

4. $10 \times 12 =$ _______

5. $10 \times 11 =$ _______

6. $5 \times 3 =$ _______

7. $5 \times 9 =$ _______

8. $5 \times 10 =$ _______

Name: _______________________________ Score: ______

1. 5 × 2 = ______

2. 5 × 4 = ______

3. 5 × 7 = ______

4. 10 × 3 = ______

5. 10 × 4 = ______

6. 5 × 8 = ______

7. 10 × 8 = ______

8. 5 × 12 = ______

MULTIPLICATION

Name: _________________________________ Score: _______

1. 5 × 8 = _______   **5.** 5 × 2 = _______

2. 5 × 12 = _______   **6.** 10 × 4 = _______

3. 5 × 5 = _______   **7.** 10 × 12 = _______

4. 10 × 11 = _______   **8.** 5 × 3 = _______

Name: _________________________________ Score: _______

1. 5 × 7 = _______

2. 5 × 11 = _______

3. 10 × 9 = _______

4. 10 × 1 = _______

5. 10 × 3 = _______

6. 10 × 10 = _______

7. 5 × 4 = _______

8. 5 × 10 = _______

MULTIPLICATION

Name: _________________________________ Score: ______

1. 10 × 7 = ______   **5.** 5 × 4 = ______

2. 10 × 5 = ______   **6.** 5 × 8 = ______

3. 10 × 8 = ______   **7.** 10 × 12 = ______

4. 10 × 6 = ______   **8.** 10 × 7 = ______

DIVISION

Name: _______________________________ Score: _______

1. $27 \div 3 =$ _______

2. $6 \div 3 =$ _______

3. $40 \div 8 =$ _______

4. $24 \div 6 =$ _______

5. $12 \div 3 =$ _______

6. $8 \div 4 =$ _______

7. $90 \div 9 =$ _______

8. $18 \div 9 =$ _______

Name: _______________________________ Score: _______

1. 28 ÷ 4 = _______

2. 21 ÷ 3 = _______

3. 42 ÷ 6 = _______

4. 14 ÷ 7 = _______

5. 32 ÷ 4 = _______

6. 4 ÷ 2 = _______

7. 10 ÷ 5 = _______

8. 36 ÷ 9 = _______

Name: _______________________________ Score: _______

1. 9 ÷ 1 = _______

2. 10 ÷ 1 = _______

3. 40 ÷ 10 = _______

4. 2 ÷ 2 = _______

5. 40 ÷ 5 = _______

6. 90 ÷ 9 = _______

7. 10 ÷ 10 = _______

8. 21 ÷ 3 = _______

Name: ________________________________ Score: ______

1. 25 ÷ 5 = ______   **5.** 36 ÷ 9 = ______

2. 3 ÷ 3 = ______   **6.** 40 ÷ 10 = ______

3. 9 ÷ 3 = ______   **7.** 35 ÷ 7 = ______

4. 56 ÷ 7 = ______   **8.** 30 ÷ 10 = ______

Name: _________________________________ Score: _______

1. $2 \div 1 =$ _______

2. $48 \div 6 =$ _______

3. $27 \div 9 =$ _______

4. $20 \div 4 =$ _______

5. $12 \div 6 =$ _______

6. $30 \div 6 =$ _______

7. $45 \div 9 =$ _______

8. $70 \div 7 =$ _______

Name: _________________________________ Score: ______

1. $2 \div 1 =$ ______

2. $3 \div 1 =$ ______

3. $30 \div 3 =$ ______

4. $60 \div 10 =$ ______

5. $72 \div 8 =$ ______

6. $18 \div 6 =$ ______

7. $30 \div 5 =$ ______

8. $40 \div 10 =$ ______

Name: _______________________________ Score: ______

1. $20 \div 5 =$ _______

2. $20 \div 2 =$ _______

3. $12 \div 3 =$ _______

4. $64 \div 8 =$ _______

5. $7 \div 1 =$ _______

6. $54 \div 6 =$ _______

7. $40 \div 5 =$ _______

8. $20 \div 10 =$ _______

Name: _________________________________ Score: _______

1. $12 \div 6 =$ _______

2. $56 \div 8 =$ _______

3. $80 \div 8 =$ _______

4. $70 \div 10 =$ _______

5. $3 \div 3 =$ _______

6. $8 \div 2 =$ _______

7. $81 \div 9 =$ _______

8. $6 \div 1 =$ _______

Name: _______________________________ Score: _______

1. $3 \div 3 =$ _______

2. $8 \div 2 =$ _______

3. $81 \div 9 =$ _______

4. $6 \div 1 =$ _______

5. $18 \div 2 =$ _______

6. $4 \div 2 =$ _______

7. $5 \times 4 =$ _______

8. $5 \times 8 =$ _______

Name: _________________________________ Score: _______

1. $10 \times 12 =$ _______

2. $10 \times 7 =$ _______

3. $5 \times 9 =$ _______

4. $5 \times 3 =$ _______

5. $6 + 3 =$ _______

6. $3 + 3 =$ _______

7. $3 + 1 =$ _______

8. $9 + 0 =$ _______

Name: _________________________________ Score: _______

1. $8 + 0 = $ _______

2. $0 + 6 = $ _______

3. $13 - 11 = $ _______

4. $12 - 1 = $ _______

5. $11 - 1 = $ _______

6. $15 - 5 = $ _______

7. $17 - 6 = $ _______

8. $19 - 4 = $ _______

ANSWERS

1. 11	**1.** 10	**1.** 62	**1.** 33	**1.** 45
2. 8	**2.** 9	**2.** 24	**2.** 15	**2.** 50
3. 12	**3.** 18	**3.** 82	**3.** 87	**3.** 20
4. 10	**4.** 8	**4.** 96	**4.** 99	**4.** 30
5. 8	**5.** 13	**5.** 15	**5.** 51	**5.** 100
6. 12	**6.** 12	**6.** 50	**6.** 86	**6.** 25
7. 8	**7.** 7	**7.** 10	**7.** 59	**7.** 10
8. 14	**8.** 16	**8.** 40	**8.** 58	**8.** 40

1. 9	**1.** 13	**1.** 71	**1.** 94	**1.** 50
2. 10	**2.** 16	**2.** 61	**2.** 72	**2.** 110
3. 11	**3.** 11	**3.** 72	**3.** 82	**3.** 55
4. 17	**4.** 11	**4.** 73	**4.** 20	**4.** 70
5. 4	**5.** 15	**5.** 94	**5.** 60	**5.** 35
6. 11	**6.** 13	**6.** 25	**6.** 35	**6.** 10
7. 9	**7.** 9	**7.** 21	**7.** 41	**7.** 60
8. 9	**8.** 10	**8.** 44	**8.** 22	**8.** 30

1. 19	**1.** 12	**1.** 35	**1.** 70	**1.** 90
2. 9	**2.** 14	**2.** 60	**2.** 33	**2.** 40
3. 16	**3.** 13	**3.** 43	**3.** 30	**3.** 20
4. 11	**4.** 9	**4.** 16	**4.** 71	**4.** 60
5. 8	**5.** 20	**5.** 37	**5.** 60	**5.** 100
6. 5	**6.** 12	**6.** 40	**6.** 63	**6.** 20
7. 17	**7.** 15	**7.** 71	**7.** 42	**7.** 70
8. 13	**8.** 8	**8.** 52	**8.** 21	**8.** 60

1. 15	**1.** 15	**1.** 45	**1.** 61	**1.** 5
2. 12	**2.** 3	**2.** 41	**2.** 68	**2.** 30
3. 15	**3.** 14	**3.** 32	**3.** 34	**3.** 55
4. 12	**4.** 10	**4.** 12	**4.** 27	**4.** 120
5. 15	**5.** 17	**5.** 95	**5.** 50	**5.** 110
6. 11	**6.** 12	**6.** 2	**6.** 43	**6.** 15
7. 12	**7.** 6	**7.** 13	**7.** 41	**7.** 45
8. 9	**8.** 20	**8.** 21	**8.** 82	**8.** 50

1.	10	1.	9	1.	2	1.	1
2.	20	2.	2	2.	8	2.	4
3.	35	3.	5	3.	3	3.	9
4.	30	4.	4	4.	5	4.	6
5.	40	5.	4	5.	2	5.	9
6.	40	6.	2	6.	5	6.	2
7.	80	7.	10	7.	5	7.	20
8.	60	8.	2	8.	10	8.	40

1.	40	1.	7	1.	2	1.	120
2.	60	2.	7	2.	3	2.	70
3.	25	3.	7	3.	10	3.	45
4.	110	4.	2	4.	6	4.	15
5.	10	5.	8	5.	9	5.	9
6.	40	6.	2	6.	3	6.	6
7.	120	7.	2	7.	6	7.	4
8.	15	8.	4	8.	4	8.	9

1.	35	1.	9	1.	4	1.	8
2.	55	2.	10	2.	10	2.	6
3.	90	3.	4	3.	4	3.	2
4.	10	4.	1	4.	8	4.	11
5.	30	5.	8	5.	7	5.	10
6.	100	6.	10	6.	9	6.	10
7.	20	7.	1	7.	8	7.	11
8.	50	8.	7	8.	2	8.	15

1.	70	1.	5	1.	2
2.	50	2.	1	2.	7
3.	80	3.	3	3.	10
4.	60	4.	8	4.	7
5.	20	5.	4	5.	1
6.	40	6.	4	6.	4
7.	120	7.	5	7.	9
8.	70	8.	3	8.	6